P9-AGI-879

WITHDRAWN
UTSA LIBRARIES

Word from the Hills

❊ WORD FROM THE HILLS ❊

A Sonnet Sequence in Four Movements

Richard Moore

University of Georgia Press
Athens

Copyright © 1972 by the University of Georgia Press

Library of Congress catalogue card number: 71-184776
International Standard Book Number: 0-8203-0287-2

Printed in the United States of America

The author and the publisher gratefully acknowledge permission to reprint the following sonnets which have previously appeared in the magazines under the titles here noted: "Country Campus" (nos. 38, 39, 40, 41, 42, 43) and "Inheritances" (nos. 3, 9, 11, 14, 15), *The Georgia Review;* "Oddball" (no. 44), *The Hollins Critic;* "Country Teacher" (nos. 22, 37), "My Father's Farm" (nos. 16, 17, 27, 28, 29, 30), "Figures in a Landscape" (nos. 6, 10, 33, 35), and "On First Looking into the Hills of Vermont" (no. 7), *Mill Mountain Review;* "Dynasty" (nos. 31, 32, 49, 50, 55, 56), *Modern Occasions;* No. 34 (untitled), *The Nation;* "Sonnet" (no. 23), *Poetry* (Chicago); *"Ad Patrem"* (nos. 1, 2, 4, 12, 13, 57, 58), *The Southern Review.*

LIBRARY
University of Texas
At San Antonio

For Janet

❋ PART I ❋

1

The wind is blowing through the blighted birch.
Its wormy leaves all toss with gay abandon.
Father, you planted it the year Alf Landon
fought for the good old days. I watch it lurch
beside your hillhouse, where you let me perch,
and still the parlor-pinks and liberals land in
the Government, the moon, this field I stand in;
the rights of man scream from each Negro church.

You loved our town, our little feudal fief
ruled by the rich grocer, accomplished thief
and friend of yours. You worshiped the same god,
and yet, father, you never tried his beef.
Now with black maggots crawling on each leaf,
your creamy birch creaks, rotten in its clod.

2

You climbed this hill when summer suns went down,
and made plans. Now it's winter. Now all year
we live among your weedy projects here:
your measured lines, your house, lawn, shrubs, the brown
leaves, crinkled like your concentrating frown,
planning to have your son an engineer.
Maybe that's why my poetry's so queer.
O father, I'm a literary clown.

You sought fixed answers, lands to plot and prune.
Only the stars are fixed. See: hills there strangle
the sun now, whose gore spills, darkens . . . and soon
the still blue heavens prematurely dangle
Jupiter, Venus, and a slice of moon.
Tonight they're an isosceles triangle.

3

This basement bargain used to be a farm.
Reliving boyhood's soft, delicious pains,
you eased your Cadillac up country lanes
and muscled in; your homespun city charm
and money stilled the natives' wild alarm.
They're mostly lunatics, our local swains.
Our neighbor's wife blew out her feeble brains
and stiffened, cradled on her husband's arm.

Snow devils dance the meadow, down the aisles
of logging trails, and up our looted alp.
A sapling stubble pricks from the white scalp
of old Bald Hill. Nothing but distance. Miles
of nothing, clear to Starky's Mountain. You,
father, tore down the barn and bared the view.

4

Nobody's here; nobody but the wind.
Over the meadow changing with the hours,
where brooks lie under snow with grass and flowers,
from time to time it blows a leaf, unpinned
from forest crowding in, undisciplined,
to fill this emptiness you say is ours.
But father, have you spoken with the powers
that haunt here now? They watched us come and grinned.

Nobody's lived here, where the road ascends
the hill and disappears—and here it ends:
a house, with a few saplings poking forth
from the lost ground below, and for their friends,
the wind and the deep cold—which buckles, bends,
and half the stone foundation inches north.

5

I climb our hill at sundown every day
to see them all come on: the neighbors' lights
in nearby valleys and, above, the night's,
as earth goes into dark and drops away.
Only the land I stand on seems to stay
and bear me still, where nothingness invites.
I walk there, never tumbling from the heights,
knowing new land will rise along my way.

Such confidence is more like that of stars,
keeping their paths through darkness, clear and pure,
than that of man, whose lonely twinkle jars
in earth's vast empty shadow, insecure.
Crossing the darkness there, see how a car's
headlights look straight ahead, just making sure.

6

Our great fat neighbor's given up his ax
for an old chainsaw. On the jobs he shirks
it's a great help, because it seldom works.
It whines like his sick wife, who aborts, lacks
vitamins, teeth. Hospitals break their backs.
Lost on the New Frontier, in the pale murks
of secondhand TV, fame, fortune lurks,
flickers, and leaves them hypochondriacs.

They stir sometimes to bring us firewood,
which helps our furnace keep the baby warm
when the wind makes us feel our parenthood
and doubt the house, and snowflakes bite and swarm.
Last New Year's Eve they climbed through such a storm
to tell us, stranded here, they understood.

7

Across three thousand miles of queasy brine
we sailed to lands my love had never seen
that the rich grocer rules as his demesne,
home of the woodchuck, skunk, and porcupine,
junkyards, collapsing farms, bordering mine,
and, father, breathing the pure air serene,
your people, pinched, insinuating, mean.
Their plundered hills have nagged them till they whine.

It's time we settled, let the children grow.
London, goodbye; goodbye, Paris and Rome!
Outside our windows arctic howlers blow
over this lunar landscape. Home sweet home:
gray tanks of bottlegas lie deep in snow
like mythic dolphins, nosing through the foam.

8

Spring brings us guests, along with dandelions—
a lowly flower, controlled in Europe, freed
to grow on our great landscape; it's a weed.
Barnabys, Blodgetts, Bilbos, and O'Briens
subdued Mohegans, Mexicans, and Mayans
and brought—along with trinket, gaud, and bead—
a dirty-pocket stowaway, a seed
tougher than prairie wolves and mountain lions.

O pioneers, dumb heroes dead and gone,
you too were commonfolk, all stalk and brawn,
who took this flower, not meaning to take it;
and sometimes I feel sad, watching your spawn
crowding in clusters on our party lawn,
that bluebells and primroses didn't make it.

9

I mow your lawn, banked steep with plough and grater;
you never tried, preferring to bespeak
yokels to do your bidding. Now the meek
inherit. Father, you old labor hater,
I serve as bottle washer, cook, and waiter
when each new baby comes and, mumbling Greek
and Latin, clean your ditches, and each week
poke in your hot, smoking incinerator.

Burn rubbish, father; drain the marshy land!
Our labor makes it ours by native right.
I sweat, make verses; you bought, built, and planned.
With the sun down and the moon up, I stand,
casting my shadow by the lesser light,
and watch my garbage glowing in the night.

10

She is the neighbor's sister's bastard daughter
adopted to these hills. No one can guess,
except Americans, what sordidness
goes with infrequent use of soap and water.
This little girl, who watches daddy slaughter
the autumn pig and has a bad abscess
in her new tooth, holes in her party dress,
and no wheels on the bike her daddy bought her—

what will become of her? In muddy boots
among the fenders, tires, and inner tubes
of daddy's junkyard, rotting without roots,
she skips, a little witch among the boobs.
This land has no use for its brightest shoots.
She'll marry, since we outlaw prostitutes.

11

You were so solid, father, cold and raw
as these north winters, where your angry will
first hardened, as the earth when the long chill
deepens—as is this country's cruel law—
yet under trackless snow, without a flaw
covering meadow, road, and stubbled hill,
the springs and muffled streams were running still,
dark until spring came, and the awful thaw.

In your decay a gentleness appears
I hadn't guessed—when, gray as rotting snow,
propped in your chair, your face will run with tears,
trying to speak, and your hand, stiff and slow,
will touch my child—who, sensing the cold years
in your eyes, cries until you let her go.

12

The Negroes riot, father, while spring's flood
loosens the earth gripped by our rigid trees,
which mark the sky with hardened arteries
growing deformed with lumps of sticky bud.
The white man's burden labors in your blood;
yearly rebellions undermine your knees. . . .
You never ventured here when winter's freeze
dissolved to deep morasses of spring mud.

See—the brown earth thaws like a Negro bride
moist with the sun, which wants her gullies bare,
and down her flanks the melting garments slide.
Violence trembles in our altered air;
slowly great landed Cadillacs subside
into the roads their tires rut and tear.

13

When hostile midges mass along the brook
and sunlight blasts the meadow, with my sore
eyes I can see you in the First World War,
father, a bright young man who'd found his nook:
you fought it safe and sound on Sandy Hook
and in those starchy uniforms you wore
courted a lady who a poet bore,
quite properly, according to the book.

Some grew rebellious when shell, mine, and bomb,
blasting in mud, touched off the nightly shriek.
Sluggards—forgive them, father, they were weak.
I too avoid exposure when the calm
heat, like the huge offensive on the Somme,
blinds me—and crouch inside here, reading Greek.

14

Old grumbling fascist, I'm the sad recorder
of your fields, mountains, and outlandish views.
Thinking corrupt democracies would lose
when Hitler's panzers crossed the Polish border,
you were first neutralist, and then a hoarder
of beef and butter, while six million Jews,
confusing issues, vanished up the flues,
and still the world lacked discipline and order.

I was in college then, grinding out bills
for you to pay, imagining what luster
I'd give your name, and using my new skills
to probe your thumping prejudice and bluster.
Now still your milk of hard-earned profit spills,
and you lie helpless as a filibuster.

15

In your great house that I can't live in yet,
where you lie failing in an upper room,
I place my middle age's seedy bloom
and wait, as the owl waits for the sunset.
I'm tired, father, of living in your debt
and, in repayment, labor to entomb
you in my bitter words, God knows for whom—
the only younger son you dared beget.

Age of monstrosities . . . I try to grieve
for your lost world, but only can conceive
your image, bristly as an armadillo,
lying in bed the night I took my leave,
pretending sleep in clumsy make-believe,
pushing your great head deeper in your pillow.

※ PART II ※

16

It's strange that no one planted trees to shade
and glorify this house in autumn, shield
it in high summer from the glaring field,
from wind in winter—strange that children played
here by the undrained marsh, grew up, decayed,
and no sign of their pleasure is revealed.
Although the land was worked, each summer's yield
harvested, did it only pass in trade,

did no one really live here? That vast ghost,
our windy hayfield overgrown with weed,
blows, as the ocean on a crumbling coast,
into our pool and garden. Do we need
such playthings, father, who can play the host
to porcupines and club them till they bleed?

17

Father or mother or lost childhood hate . . .
or were there passions, now too faint to name,
evilly present here before they came,
that mere rebuilding won't eradicate?
Your fall here, father, and that smoking grate
at midnight, breaking into sudden flame—
but most the fall—as if some fright or shame
around the stairs blurred, made you hesitate. . . .

The owner didn't live here, even then—
only his tenants, forlorn shiftless men
with bitter wives, who staked their savings, failed,
and pleased the owner, who could sell again.
You flushed him, father, drained the cellar fen.
In the new stairs your own collapse was nailed.

18

The curse here is intensest near the house.
Sometimes I climb the hills to lighter air
and, almost microscopic, see it there,
dug into meadow, fastened, a white louse
that jumped from the soft cloth of woods, the blouse
which cloaks the mounds nearby, and notice where,
with its mowed lawn, it sucks the meadow bare,
or seems to. My imported English spouse,

three charming children (one as yet unborn)
and house cat move, perhaps before my eyes,
invisible as seeds of yearly corn
that used to grow there. All shrinks down to size. . . .
We came from gladder landscapes; now we mourn
a seed that grows. It is our soil that dies.

19

Under the moon's nightly increasing sliver
I pace through summer. On our hilltop road
after the weeds are pulled, the garden hoed,
the family outing to Mosquito River,
sweet evening comes to chill me, and I shiver
and think about the cautious mouse and toad
bold in our weedy meadow, still unmowed,
soon to be house cat—stomach, brain, and liver.

Our cat's pregnant. She needs those little things.
Deep in the grasses each doomed cricket sings
under the swelling moon, shining so sweetly
that all my constellations—heroes, kings,
Berenice's hairdo and Aquila's wings
and the Great Swan—are glittered out completely.

20

Desire has failed this evening, and the dead
hills of our lunar landscape wane and wane
through summers, busy once with milk and grain.
At nightfall, up the rutting roads which led
to farms, beer bottles on their stony bed
say that a great excitement ends in pain.
A car starts and pulls out of lover's lane,
limps down the hill, its tail lights glowing red.

Back to the house, its lights out, floating dark—
for everyone must touch and hug his own;
and fumbling up the unseen lane to park,
everyone finds somewhere his bed of stone.
They hate it here; then let them leave my Ark,
and let me stay and find this place alone.

21

From dreams tormented by our house in flames
I wake at noon to hear my butterfly,
my sudden golden flower, vilify
her image, her small daughter, with screamed names,
because we pin her here, because she blames
my indolence, which lets her stultify
with no companions but the windowed sky
and the dark mirrors, hung in antique frames.

There's me, the new, angry inheritor,
whom she can feel, dimly aware of her
sometimes. Sometimes she's beautiful; but here
the antiques can't remember what we were
in furnished rooms—where every flatterer
filled her with joy, and me with hate and fear.

22

from a mean college that seems made for me
In this amazing land, where I can get
it's been three frigid winters since my pet
money for talking about poetry,
has had a satisfactory hairset
or husband. Anyone, she says, can see
I've lost that gentle sensitivity
she said was weakness in the year we met.

A grumpy father, fighting for a place
in a dead world, forgets his year of grace
tramping the windy downs, a quaint nobody
blest with a native wife and time to pace
Homer's hexameters in lonely study,
at home with the lost Adam of his race.

23

She had no choice; worn out by the Comtesse
whose dog she walked, drawn by that little car
I had in France, my dearest has gone far,
to reincarnate in this plundered mess
that in the good old days was wilderness,
where she can question the unlucky star
that told her not to wait for a Jaguar,
but pity a poor ego in distress.

Cassandra, Agamemnon's foreign bride,
feeling the pressure of Apollo's call
though ignorant, the day her captor died
among his trivia perceived it all—
the pompous king, the family curse inside,
the car empty before the palace wall.

24

Earth will not tolerate too many lives.
When a young hemlock, shapely to the eye,
is two, grown tight together, one will die,
while one, misshapen by the loss, survives.
Some say that when a human child arrives
a saintliness occurs; we know they lie.
And The Lord said, Increase and multiply;
we know what cruelties The Lord contrives.

And so we tampered with life's sacred source,
and knifed into the mystery, and hired
the work, and answered the Life Force with force.
It was unnatural; she felt remorse,
and having done what she herself desired,
she wept some, then signed up for an art course.

25

No wonder that sometimes she shouts defiance;
for she, who thinks grandly and most admires
great souls imposing as cathedral spires,
must now endure a literary giant's
mean spirit, full of thrift and self-reliance—
were these the virtues that through miles of wires
screamed from another state his sick desires,
shocking her through those miracles of science?

Though she, once gay, once elegantly styled,
must now participate in marriage crimes
in which both strangle, mutually reviled,
other things please her now, like saving dimes,
like children's games. She knows the nursery rhymes
forgotten here, and sings them to a child.

26

After the nastiness of a black mood,
squeezing the rancor of our marriage out
until it burst, splattering in a shout
that rang far in our upland solitude,
two deer, bent to the grasses that they chewed,
looked up at the strange house, and seemed in doubt,
and stared a moment still, then wheeled about,
puff tails bobbing, as if the voice pursued.

Sometimes at parties—joking, I suppose—
I say "Deer frighten me," and people scoff.
They've never sat silent in khaki clothes,
sunk in the deep forest, and had to cough
politely to inform three charging does
a man was breathing there and scare them off.

27

I know that a way out has to be found
soon, before wife and babies grow disloyal,
from here, where gray rocks are the only spoil
miraculously appearing above ground,
thrust out of its slow depths without a sound—
but where to next? Is there more fertile soil,
another shabby college somewhere? Toil
into the restless deeps, lest ye be drowned!

And now, guessing what father's land is worth,
I grow stone dull, she says, and ill at ease.
Can this poor soul endure one more rebirth?
O slow, slow through the yearly thaw and freeze
the buried boulders stagger to their knees,
break through the sod, but cannot leave this earth.

28

One day at nightfall, when thick fog revealed,
by barbed wire fence, a tree trunk, more or less,
which dripped out of its upper nothingness
into a lane and cattle-gutted field,
and even the near neighbor's lights were sealed
behind a mask of space and timelessness,
leaving the desolation to confess
a fender, lying like a broken shield—

like war, I thought—the horror fields of France.
A shell hole, once a ploughed-out cattle pond,
confronted me . . . and when I tried to lance
my flashlight beam, waving it like a wand,
into the drifting mist and break the trance,
it pointed nowhere. Nothing was beyond.

29

Somehow it's better with a roof of cloud
at rainy nightfall, when the streams come near,
roaring beyond the meadow, rough and clear,
and seem to bring the neighbor's cowbells, loud
from the next valley, where the cattle crowd
for warmth under a giant maple, peer
with great brown eyes at his dark farm, and hear
slow dripping leaves under the quiet shroud

which covers them and all the fading land:
whose hilltops, gone already in the mist,
suggest, to those watchers who'd understand,
that all this ceiling'd spaciousness will twist
soon, like a vapor through the grasping hand—
ghostly, too insubstantial to exist.

30

There is a house, bought before prices rose,
where old fools or young poets can retire.
Natives in nearby shacks are cheap to hire,
being without hope, food, or proper clothes.
There was a time when under winter snows
life trickled here—when there was fire
in iron stoves above the cellar mire,
which smelled as usual and never froze.

And there's an oozing squalor in our souls
which no power, no wealth, no discipline,
no mortised wall of fitting rhyme, controls.
And now, where creeping timberlands begin
that have long filled forgotten cellar holes,
we businessmen from town are digging in.

❊ PART III ❊

31

Unable, father, still, to disavow
your stable world on two great girders trussed,
sexual continence and money lust,
I too have fingered the domestic plough
and sought with guile and fervor to endow
children with life and more than a bread crust;
and that is why, lazy and broke, I must
come pussyfooting to your sickroom now.

We're simple folk; beyond our gravel road
the populations of the world explode,
but we're contented with our modest portion.
Be happy—your ancestral line's been towed;
be glad—we've done our best to ease the load:
we've had one birth here, father, one abortion.

32

Abortions should be legal, let me warn.
My mother with me, taking awful chances,
doing her best under the circumstances,
sickened with drugs, poor dear, and I was born.
No diplomat, mother would often mourn
my fits of stuttering, my childish trances,
my bizarre deeds at school and teen-age dances,
wondering what those pills had maimed or torn;

and told me the whole story, late one night,
me, drawing her on, laying careful traps,
each with its subtle bait; each time she'd bite—
and I—who draw my father's slow collapse
through lofty sonnets now—what will I write
for you, dear mother? Limericks perhaps.

33

Natty old Jenks, who, having married well
and won the store with the town's harelipped prize,
staunchly believe in bold Free Enterprise;
who didn't spare yourself—nor dared rebel
through tongue-lashed seasons, till she sank to Hell
forty years later—you epitomize
that self control, sweet in your Maker's eyes,
which makes men mighty when they buy and sell;

and now in sun-warmed Florida you've won
a second bride at sixty, blond and brown,
while fighting hard to keep school spending down
here in the cold north—where your harelipped son
carries out groceries with his pants undone
and owns the store. But you own half the town.

34

It took TV to civilize our village
and bring our stubbled codgers up to date.
Up skyscrapers new notions percolate;
into our channeled valley drips the spillage,
where junkyards cover fields once used for tillage.
Our means are modest, but the needs are great
that softly sung commercials can create.
Some call it enterprise; I call it pillage.

When every crank and far-flung solipsist
knows about Prell and Dristan Nasal Mist,
who doubts the unity of Western Culture?
Tuned to elections, watching babies kissed,
viewing with awe the murdered anarchist,
what lone Promethean liver needs a vulture?

35

He has no bathtub, but we can't ignore
our neighbor and his new private street light.
It's automatic with the fall of night
and guides his drunken steps through every chore
and turns his dark to day and, what is more,
colors his sunsets bottle-greenish white.
On clear evenings the stars shrink out of sight,
lost in the urban glare outside his door.

Southward and southward fly the summer birds,
unnoticed by our youthful Elmer Snerds,
who have their wheels to turn, their nuts to tighten,
and aren't inclined to fasten things with words,
or even look and let their muzzles brighten
at the queer flocks that, once unknown, will frighten.

36

Lyndon, our chief of men, who through a cloud
not of death only, but elections rude,
guided by guile and shameless platitude,
thy way to huge majorities hast ploughed,
and on the neck by bumptious Barry cowed,
hast reared thy trophies and thy work pursued,
riding with Hubert, that ferocious dude,
while columnists resound thy praises loud:

Milton deserts me now; yet much remains
besides the memory of Bobby Baker.
We've seen a leader with style, verve, and brains
shot down: a pity if his ghost complains
that the bold brightness of an image-maker
is clouded by a dull consensus-taker.

37

Though the new teacher is a trifle odd,
the nuns are kind to me: never condemn
my heresies, nor know what bile and phlegm
stir up the student seedlings in my pod.
Through *Paradise Lost* yearly we still plod,
dwelling with love on each poetic gem.
I do my utmost to conceal from them
poetry's vilest monster, Milton's God.

It's risky, fathers, to send girls to school
these days, where they, neglecting things divine,
might listen to a poet, who will fool
away their hours, trying to define
innocence, gone when babes no longer drool,
and how it feels to club a porcupine.

38

The university library, bright
in all its portholes, all of its watts burning,
a ship of fools, a vast dreadnought of learning,
voyages hugely on the campus night.
I feel mortification at the sight,
I, mothlike on the football field, discerning
heads bent, bent on increased powers of earning,
and collared scholars, fumbling in the light—

those stacks of plenty, now too much for us.
What tender mind resists that stately gleam,
that treasure house, in which (expressing thus,
America, the sweetness of your dream)
four separate periodicals discuss
the sale and manufacture of ice cream?

39

Busby, whose verse no piercing beams, no rays
can penetrate, whom dark dogmas enchant
to speak in tongues, all telling us you can't
live without Christ and critical essays—
come, pour the whiskey, swell your tongue and glaze
your eye with eloquence, until I grant
your greatness, who so gorgeously can rant
at the sick world, which will not pay, nor praise.

Is there no place, then, where the sacred tongue
can buzz in magazines—flies on the dung
which spreads to fertilize the fallow masses?
Then try the quarterlies: moving among
the select few, still willing to be stung,
they trot the field, lofty as horses' asses.

40

Van Delph, after a life rich in creation
of far too many verses, you've been hired
to that professorship you've long desired,
having now long forgotten the elation
of writing lines that stirred your generation.
All hearts, but not one high paid fool, were fired,
and to a rich man's college you've retired
to tend your garden and your reputation.

The Great Society has found a place
even for that rapacious snapping crowd,
the dying conscience of our dying race,
and philistine reviewers grow less loud,
calling the Ivory Tower a disgrace,
now that on every campus it's endowed.

41

Ivy League Teack, our Air Force hero, smitten
with peace no less than war, who now can raid
icecaps for fame and mythic beasts and wade
through polar lakes, losing your shirt and mitten;
whom all animals love, except our kitten,
for you're a gentle scholar undismayed
by strength, a brilliant author who've been paid
three times for two fine books you've never written:

drumming up projects, cultivating takers
with cash to spend, doubtless you never will,
lording it on your thousand bank-owned acres
and vegetating on your private hill:
idealist still, once one of our earth-shakers,
medaled for bombing towns with deadly skill.

42

Flayton, who've come with your sound tracks, guitar
and homemade mandolin to find the folk,
with our town witches, long gone up in smoke:
ballad collector, sickly wild-eyed star
of plucked nostalgia, need one move this far
to find a fresh-air slum and have a stroke?
Now you must stick to scholarship and soak
a bearded drunk who owns a racing car.

He needs a fellow hepcat who can care,
and you're your brother's keeper and his heir . . .
while in a hillside shack our local louse-
infested singer of old songs, aware
he'd be unwelcome in your modern house,
gurgles his tawdry tunes to empty air.

43

Richard, while Flayton labored for our school
and had a heart attack and he and Teack,
loving this town, rose in its hall to speak
against its grocer's sly exploiting rule,
you spent the spring, digging a pleasant pool
deep in your backyard brook, reading more Greek,
and writing nasty poems in a pique,
covering useful men with ridicule.

Why do you rankle at their eager ilk?
You're not at all like them. You meanly hanker
Van Delph's professorship and mean to milk
your father's land to feed your wormy rancor,
producing lines as elegant as silk,
and, when you've finished, sell out to a banker.

44

Oswald, you did what I would never dare
and killed a President: the one with style
we cheered and left unmurdered for a while,
charming old countries, young and debonaire,
whom Congress could ignore, with his strange flair
for quoting poets and his boyish smile.
Dallas seemed suited for a deed that vile,
that stoned another statesman speaking there,

but it was you, with hatreds like my own,
only not schooled, like mine, to mockery.
For days your innocence so clearly shone
in your blurred face, dying on our TV,
in such confusion, how could I have known
that you'd have murdered him, that you were me?

※ PART IV ※

45

Blest be the midnight thaw among the signs
of spring, when one can dress in lighter stuffs
and walk the muddy roads without earmuffs,
noting more nakedly how the wind whines
cantabile through orchestras of pines
as the young moon in hiding scatters puffs
of tarnished silver, which the wind rebuffs,
shaping the darkness to its soft designs.

I've seen those lights in sleep, or nearing sleep,
out of my inner darkness sometimes seep
and curl in driven clouds before they flee,
vanishing into heaven knows what deep,
and wondered when, if ever, I shall see
what moon may hide in cloudy depths of me.

46

Sometimes at sundown distant hills take hold
of our west mountain rim and climb no higher
than wrinkled dwarfs or pigmies would require
to see our world under their sunset gold.
Fixed in that amber sky, they seem as old
as the earth's age of rock and lava fire,
crouching, a sooty silent little choir,
where the earth's mountains open, fold on fold.

But soon the eastern sky, sown with its grain
of stars, darkens, and they will not remain,
those pigmies filing to their hunt, long after,
though their sky covers with a crimson stain,
an image of some long forgotten pain,
on which they linger, crumpled up with laughter.

47

Few of us know they're here, and fewer care,
our first natives, whose skin, the tint of dirt,
blends with our woods so well, and bodies, girt
with the fresh hides of porcupine and bear,
give even sober foresters a scare.
Molesting no one, they remain unhurt.
In spring they smear their bodies with skunk-squirt;
people have often fled them, unaware.

The Indians, more primitive than we,
noticed them—first taught them those furtive habits.
We never found them; yet in tracery
of moonlit woods, they have appeared to me,
and their live eyes, hunting their friends, the rabbits,
watch, as the stars do, our whole history.

48

I often think about these twilight years
of mass murders and race-staggering crimes
and slower death in empty pantomimes
of sentiment, from which a horror leers;
but most I think of one recorded queer's
velvety vocals, who a thousand times
has crooned emasculated nursery rhymes
into our daughters' young and helpless ears.

In the beginning men were not estranged
from the earth spirits. Shelterless and dumb
over uncultivated lands they ranged,
uncursed by crooners. To the hollow drum
century followed century unchanged,
and men knew what their daughters would become.

49

Forgive those disagreeable surprises
that you engendered with your second son,
father: the monstrous things he's said and done,
which after thirty years he recognizes.
In spite of all rich fatherhood devises
to standardize its product, once the fun
is over, father, see the gamuts run.
We don't come in convenient shapes and sizes.

Civilization is at fault. Deep dells
of lofty words entice the young romancer
from healthy things. But why do loyal cells,
caught in a dying body, have no answer
to the corruption when that one rebels
to save its life and multiplies to cancer?

50

A blackbird squats down in our gully wood
and cries out at its echo or its mate:
a grating cry, hungry and full of hate.
I heard it as a boy and understood,
savored and swallowed it as best I could,
and still it squawked, refusing to abate,
against my wife, my father, and my fate.
Father, I have that blackbird's hardihood.

I've watched a rural Eden go kaput.
I'll be at home in good old city soot.
Your woods are threadbare, father, dark and stormy,
and full of ugly beasts that won't stay put.
We've monsters here: I've but to stamp my foot
on our dirt road, and they all flee before me.

51

Old shadow moon, dark eyeball with new lens,
who look at the sunk sun, from whom you've tapped your
luminous presence, help me to recapture
the lost thoughts of my pigmies; for when men's
quick souls danced with the gods in jungle dens,
sages of Egypt spoke of them with rapture,
but you, who touched their wild eyes, also lapped your
glow on these hills and once uncattled fens.

Let them appear with hair kinky or curled
and say: Man is no more than what he touches;
nor was he less until Hephaestus, twirled
out of the sky from Zeus's upstart clutches,
pulled magic rabbits out of hats and hutches—
at which God squatted and produced The World.

52

With its great belly heaving, cracked and bruised
from the frost's push, sore from the ice's sting,
slowly the earth emerges into spring.
Under the brook-loud hills today, it oozed
at every step, and not a sod refused
my boot's print. Long imprisoned waters swing
out over sunny meadows, glittering.
The dark tunnels beneath cave in, unused.

What if they do, father? See: dying sun,
striking across the hillsides, has begun
to shape with shadows every mound and hummock.
No one can guess what the deep frost has done.
From steps on the dry road, dark trickles run;
stiff gravel gives, like walking on a stomach.

53

Gee-gees were horses, *ta-ta* her first word
for her dark faeces, when through hay and heather
toddling, we stopped to see, as dry as leather,
a heap of lumps, a hummock of horse turd;
and, *Da?* she questioned, who had only heard
meaningless names till then—when like a feather
a thought struck and I put her words together,
not once daring to hope for what occurred:

she stood there, silent, puzzled, open-eyed,
as if I'd handed her some shiny token,
then, *Gee-gee ta-ta . . . gee-gee ta-ta!* cried,
as if a shell surrounding her had broken,
and shouted still, till all the hills replied—
till the dark hills surrounding us had spoken.

54

My dear, my dancer, to these clumsy feet
wedded of mine, trip from this troubled page
lightly as ever through our twilight age,
where love and death are still not obsolete,
and bring one daughter, fiery and petite
like you, and one like me, quiet, with sage
twinkles and thoughts impossible to gauge,
but plump with songs and all things good to eat,

and spread a picnic blanket on the ground
and fill forests of summer with your cries
and quickly now, before the leaves have browned,
make them like you, and not like him who lies
pregnant with ghosts, while shadows all around,
astir with leaves, twinkle with impish eyes.

55

The village idiot's soft saintly smile,
delicate features, and calm noble face,
flashed on my vision once, will not erase,
though vision blurs and other sights defile;
for it contained no turpitude, no guile,
that emptiness, and there I seemed to trace
hints of lost years, thinking that such a race
might have survived on earth a little while.

But no; he's cultivated; he's like you,
father: the failing moonlight, not the new;
for when the first powerful pioneer
struck down our trees, from the destruction grew
cities, but from the man, still planted here,
our palest flower, this empty residue.

56

In your great shadowed house in the moonlight
one window shines above your private park.
You're dying, father, and you fear the dark.
Maybe you lie awake and think tonight
how once, magnificent in appetite,
among peculiar fish a mighty shark,
you cruised Manhattan's depths and left your mark:
founders of houses aren't always polite.

Dynasties pass, leaving their psychic scars,
with or without descendants who recanted,
having consumed the energies they're granted.
Though we were rascals, father, nothing mars
one image now: the dark hemlocks you planted
striding above me past a million stars.

57

In the great storms of autumn, when cold spills
into our valley, and trees, brittle-boughed
from drought of the late summer, crack aloud
and rattle their last leaves; when the wind kills
the nests and hutches, which the blizzard fills,
and faint lights flee from cloud to southward cloud—
only the trees remain, bare and wind-ploughed.
Who will pronounce the darkness of the hills?

A man is needed here, not to destroy
or build, only to listen to the wind
and be the wind. Sometimes a girl or boy
is as the stormy moonlight disciplined,
and as blown seed, and fathoms laws of joy
and sorrow revolutions won't rescind.

58

A few sick crickets still—that's all of summer—
under Orion, rising in the east.
Each chilling day our daylight is decreased—
draining away, and no one calls a plumber;
and who'll adjust my ribcaged, my blind drummer,
beating me nowhere? Here, far from the feast,
one learns the death of a few weeds at least;
seasons grow slowly clear to the newcomer.

As summer cloud shadows' enormous flight
over the hills, now wind reverberates.
The warmth is gone; I'm finished with debates.
Soon snow will come: recovered from its blight,
father, your empty birch in the starlight,
with all its fallen leaves around it, waits.